CITYSCAPES

AND OTHER POEMS

Neil Leadbeater

ISBN: 978-81-19228-74-4

First Edition: 2023
Rs. 200/-

Cyberwit.net
HIG 45 Kaushambi Kunj, Kalindipuram
Allahabad - 211011 (U.P.) India
http://www.cyberwit.net
E-mail: info@cyberwit.net

Printed at Vocre.

For Jane

Contents

I: Twelve Norwegian Poems

The Young Running in Bergen

Running in Bergen they've never had it so good. Eyes holding
within their sight the landlocked, shoulder-blade hills or swerving
over tram lines
down to the harbours and quays to keep a tally on noonday ships
newly-arrived at anchor after days spent apart

because seeing the alchemy of engineering makes them appreci-
ate all the more

common objects at home:

Nike fuel bands, seasonal caps, footwear for those in the know.

The young enjoying the outdoor life: grass hurdling beneath their feet:
everything pushing with an equal force: hard stone, friction of road,
driving them upward, propelling them on:
the immense flexion of lower limbs
air vaulting the ribcage,
one foot set in front of the other

with the body in forward lean.

A Bergen Alphabetum

A slew of yellow oilskins.
Bridles. Bergen rain. Bights – loops of rope, wire or chain.
Creel haulers. Corkline. City of seven hills.
Drift nets.
Echo sounders detecting shoals.
Freezer trawlers. Funicular rails.

Ground rope. Tow rope.
Head rope.
In the harbour. In situ.
Journeys out and journeys back.
Krill.
Large-scale ocean currents. Ludwig Holberg inspecting a tramcar.
Midwater long-liners. Marshmallow light.
Net drums.
Otter boards. Ole Bull in the park. Oceanography in the North Atlantic
Pole and line vessels.
Quarterdecks.
Roll-On / Roll-Off ferries. Refrigerated tanks.
Straight-talkers who struggle with metaphor.
The city at anchor.
Umbrellas in the rain. Frames of reference for the weather.
Vivier tanks.
Warp wires. Windjammers. Winches.
XL shipping containers
Y-tracks for reversing engines
Zephyr jerseys. Zip-neck tops.

Bergen Rain

Rain is
moving in
from the west.
There will be
frequent
downpours,
heavy at times,
especially
around
coastal areas.

No wonder
we have words
for it:
regn,
regnskyll,
regnskur...
and then this
word *opplett* –
Bergen slang
for that brief
pause
before the next
rain falls.

Voss

Such a small syllable   winging its vocals
between extreme sports and skydiving clouds
in the adrenalin capital of Norway
Voss in Vestland
      wave or sea or fox.

The mountains chatter
at the edge of their ridges
the all-above, wide-awake sky-talk of birds
an April rising.

A coach disgorges birders,
the journey from Bergen
a steep-sided
jaw-dropper
that heart-in-the-mouth climactic.

After lunch, the photo stop:
snow-capped mountains, forests, lakes
fast-flowing, whitewater rivers
and this white-throated dipper
Cinclus cinclus,
Norway's national bird
flying through an aperture
with that special whirring sound.

Dusk

Seen in the last few moments:
pied flycatchers strung on a zipline,
a siege of common cranes,
a pygmy of the family *Strigidae*
hole-nesters in the boreal woods
Europe's smallest owl.

Stalheim

Traversed *one of the most dangerous roads in Northern Europe*
nerves-all-a-jangle
13 hairpins, the gradient brutal
in a coach with a careful driver.

And later over dinner in the hotel dining room
with stunning views over the Nærøy Valley
the waitress tells me between serving guests
the name of the mountain with the oval-shaped top.

Struggling to spell it,
'*O*', I said.

Gudvangen

The feeling you get canoeing a narrow fjord
hemmed in between mountains
waterfalls keeling towards you
white-water scupper-holes
in a rush, in a down-knot,
footwells, bulkheads, decklines,
a group of us in a pod, a swarm, a flock
salt in us yet.

Tomorrow there will be excursions.

Oslo

City of shipbrokers, shipping companies, maritime insurance,
Merino zip neck jumpers, utility field jackets, bulkhead sheet bags,
polyester fender ropes, marine storage fogging oil,
quicksilver storage seal, splicing needles,
bilge cleaners, shock cords, diesel fuel,
barter for steerage,
legs unsteady on solid ground
when you first set foot
on land.

Docks in the Port of Oslo

It's here where you wonder if there's a collective noun for
mechanised cranes
whether it's a cluster or a convocation,
a *perpetuum mobile* of moving cargo
shifting overhead.

You weigh it all up in your mind
a heavy burden you can't put your finger on
the dead weight of it
when empty.

Frogner

Did all these figures
walk into the park
like us
and then stand still
not wanting to move
not wanting to
not wanting?

Something must have
kept them there.
It must have come
at a beautiful moment
considering their
positions
relative to each other:
how they became
statuesque.

Stavanger

Before it was turned into a boom town
and oil replaced canning
as the city's major industry,
coffee was the focus of our attention –
not the fish, nor even the shipyards-
but the way the sets were packed in bubble wrap
before being boxed and labelled
Stavanger Flint A S Norway
pottery tableware to Handle with Care
and then, before leaving,
the thought of steeped coffee
(viscous with a hint of fruit)
to satisfy our thirst.

Ulvik

After stumbling a long time over impossible trails:
the long look down the valley
that fjord
      unforgettable

a golden ocean of barley.

II: Interlude

Our First Voyages with Ohthere and Wulfstan

That autumn in North London
when we opened Sweet's Anglo-Saxon Reader
at *Ohthere sæde his hlaforde, Ælfrede cyninge...*
it was a foray into a foreign language
and we needed to get our bearings.
Years later, I still recall *he nysse hwæðer*
when Ohthere wasn't sure if
'the land turned due south or the sea went into the land'.

By the time we got to Wulfstan
we had begun to learn how to bail out our mistakes
and after those initial flounderings,
to tack against the wind.

The precision of rendering Alfredian prose
into Modern English
left little room for manoeuvre.
We were trying to find our sea legs
or, moving on land, calm the motions of waves
rolling their weight through our stride.

III: Cityscapes, Soundscapes and the Thought of Random Lists

What I Remember About Helsinki

The shallow harbour
which meant we had to drop anchor
some way out in the bay.
That fabulous sunset over the city
seen through a porthole
the joy of getting to know a street plan
of walking on solid ground
next day.

Sisu or the art of putting on a show of courage
of cracking ice for a morning swim.

How my father went off in search of the Olympic Stadium
The monumental central station
with lines crossing to Khrushchev's Russia.

The tall post office building
Engel's neoclassical facades
the Lutheran Cathedral with its five green domes
and the statues of the twelve apostles
(How did they get there?)
Marimekko, Lumni Accessories and Vietto,
the market Square in the south arm of the bay.

Getting lost in Stockmann's.
Trying to cross the road without getting run over.

Writing this.

What I Like about Helsinki Now

Tall windows that let in the light when the sun hardly sets at all.
Handmade crafts from Lokal
not quite a gallery and not just a shop
opened in 2012.
Coffee at IPI
slow-cooked spelt porridge served daily
with homemade granola and jam.
Sipping a Bear Hug at Nord-T
quality loose-leaf blended herbs fresh from the Finnish forest.
browsing through vinyl at Digelius Music
Enjoying art at Amos Rex.
Sledding in winter.
Tucking into Sashimi Salads at the Boom Room.
Swimming in the Allan Sea Pool.
Buying cakes at Café Fleuriste
the flowers long gone from the business.
Jopo bikes from Hanko.
Winter runs pounding the bay.
Alvar Aalto's vases.
Töölö's iconic buildings.

Eating a *blini* in the heart of winter.
Dropping in to La Reine.
Seeing RELANDERSGRUND
the red vessel in the blue bay with
white buildings beyond.
Washing rugs on the waterfront
with a bucket of Baltic water.
Foraging for berries.

Living quietly when the days are short.
Wirkkala glassware. Artek chairs.
Buying shoes at Good Kicks
Footwear for the streets.

Postage on this Poem has already been Paid

In the photograph
I am standing outside the post office
in a red shirt, brown pullover
and beige trousers
wearing shades.

It is August 1964
and stamps are beginning their journeys
on postcards round the world:

a crowned lion on a red field,
lumberjacks, astronomers,
historic anniversaries,
pillars of domestic industry:

woodwork, paper
and forest administration,
banks of commerce and trade.

The opening of the Saima Canal,
feudal arms and transport,
Oskar Merikanto, Armas Järnefelt,

EUROPA stamps,
Arabia of Finland dinnerware.

Aleksis Kivi Steps Down from His Statue

Tired of sitting with his back to the theatre,
Kivi gets up and goes for a walk.

Now all his works are classics,
it's time to live in the moment.

Aulis Sallinen Enlarging the World

Listening to 'Washington Mosaics', Don Quixote tilting at windmills
or your sixth excursion into symphonic sound –
'From A New Zealand Diary'
I think of you on different continents
unleashing and controlling untameable forces
a composer far from home.

In the third movement
even the dross in the quarry bed is panned for what it is worth
as a distant and more prosperous past
wells up in 6/8 time
from the dancefloor of the earth.
The triumphant finale, headed up by a quote from Curnow
sends shockwaves down the spine:
Simply by sailing in a new direction / You could enlarge the world.

Gert Mortensen Engaging in a Dialogue with the Malmö Symphony Orchestra

You are the solo percussion player. David against Goliath, fired-up
in that ready-for-anything, red-bloodied attitude.

The orchestra pitches in
defiant with its descending scale of strings and woodwind
answered back by the vibraphone. A snarl from a split gourd
sends the opponents reeling.
Brass enters the fray
but you drown them out with a relentless battery of percussion.

End of Round One.

Successively you manage to beat them into submission –
an orchestra that tries to shrug things off
by waltzing round the podium
and then, when that fails, by voicing a theme on soaring strings.
Once more you go on the offensive.
We sense the mayhem,
muffled but real,
roiling beneath the surface.

No-one is going to give in.

Let's Go To Lahti (I)

Let's go to Lahti on the Z train
to think outside of the box
where the parcels market at Stora Enso
is bigger than any of us ever thought:
a steady flow of corrugated board
cut to shape and custom-branded
enough to stretch end to end
from Amsterdam to Brussels
every single day.
After lunch at Piano Pavilion
if there's time enough left over
there's Lahti Art for posters
or Riku Routo's motorcycles,
his red-bricked museum.

Let's Go To Lahti (II)

Let's go to Lahti
to draw ourselves up to our full height
beside the high transmission masts
standing tall on Radio Hill...
let's absorb the atmospherics,
through the background noise:
AM, FM and shortwave,
satellite, ham and walkie-talkie...
place our fingers in our ears,
say *'ephphatha'*
to hear more clearly
all those audio sounds.

The Run Through Porvoo

Welcome to Porvoo
home to renewable diesel, underground tanks,
petrochemical complexes,
kerosene, diesel and jet fuel.
To Bilfinger Nordics
for engineering and project management.
To Ensto for smart solutions.
To the traffic, shop and food trade,
Taiga Colours and Finform.
To refrigeration systems
for ventilation and air conditioning
To Brunberg Chocolate for Alku caramels,
jelly sweets and truffles
and Finnish champions, Borgå Akilles,

playing bandy in the Bandyliiga.

Freight Waiting for the Green Light

All types of cargo are here:
Ro-Ro, Lo-Lo, dry bulk, liquid bulk, gas
and project shipments.

Its industry draws you in,
the solid presence of rectangular blocks,
red like ore ranged against the quays,
the whole weight of it out in all weathers,
sitting there
with the noise of machinery
pounding in one ear and out the other,
and further on,
the tight mosaic of motor vehicles
standing in line for days at a time
stationary in the fields.

Docks in the Gulf of Finland

Observe the iron resolve of sturdy moorings,
hawsers, bollards, fenders,
catch the odour of oil and pitch,
the resin of sawn logs
dry bulk and break bulk
from Hietanen South and Hamina,
high-sided vessels rising out of dock water
that leave you small in their shadow…
the whole effort of looking up
at cargo being moved,
its bulk swung at the press of a switch
cranes stronger than any of us
where automation rules.

Writ in Nostalgia for Tampere

For those Tammerkoski rapids cascading through the park.
For children clawing at spider nets, whooshing down slides,
carefree on swings.
For mothers reaching for hampers, picnics of
strawberries and cream.
For Viktor Jansson's sculptures in Sorsapuisto Park.
For ducks, geese and swans.
For the 'Dancing Girl' so full of movement
you can almost see blue earthenware
escaping from the ground.
For white waterlilies and perfoliate pondweed.
For crowberries, bilberries and buckthorn.
For lovely landscapes, outdoor trails, fields in active use.
For Moomins everywhere.

Poem Out of Oulu

Madetoja's sound world –
that long *lento misterioso* in Opus 29
static yet captivating
played out from Oulu
bringing with it larch mists of the running wave
sprung moss underfoot
still air and soaked bark
water you could squeeze from a wringer
motionless moments
where the scent of resin after rain
rises up to meet you:
those two notes *restrained and austere*
ON / OFF, ON/ / OFF,
sounding their insistency
to ships out at sea.

Postcards from Rovaniemi

Could be Santa Claus Land.
Opening the curtains one morning
he found the road and the buildings opposite
caught in the depth of winter. Reindeer everywhere.
It would not always be like this –
you had to catch the moment
of pure undriven snow,
of St Nicholas wanting to give every child
the white wonder of Christmas.

*

Afternoons listening to Bach cantatas -
Widerstehe doch der Sünde
that edgy offbeat introduction to number 54
that only someone with the genius of Bach
could pull off to perfection.
<the tension between the tonic and diminished seventh
drives the movement>
the sleeve note said
and he mused that it was not unlike
the opening of the sixth Brandenburg -
a concerto without violins.

*

The windows give on to the white trees.
For a long time he looks at them.
What kind of trees they are we are never told.
Maybe they are not trees at all

but metaphors for something else.
[Insert what you would like them to be].

*

In the living room
his daughters are learning the art of folding paper
so many facets to their different sides.

*

His wife in the kitchen opening blinds.
Who first let light into his house.

IV: Polders and Other Poems

Bosschaert's 'Vase with Flowers'

The painting bursts with summer flowers:
colour is everywhere, curled petals splashed with green,
striations of spotted scarlets, red flames, cool blues,
and yellow suns.

Asleep between shifts
I imagine him dreaming of the Rosa Mundi
or conjuring up De Busbecq's tulips
acquired 'at great price'.

Fully awake now,
he returns to work on his 'vase'
decides to add insects as an afterthought

stands back…then smiles.

Cuyp's Cows

Suppose he never intended to paint them
and they just lumbered in,
hale, hardy and udder-heavy
in readiness for milking,
or lay down near Maas
with Dordrecht in the distance,
quiet in atmosphere and grand in appearance
to the enormous appeal
of the English.
Maybe this was how they won him over
propelling him on with his brushwork
not too fussed about taking on
the life and soul of the party.

Cows in the Evening Sun

One August in Ameland
pitched against an incredible sunset
you wished would never go down
you came across a herd of cows
nudging blades
with their rubbery tongues
eyes down to the ground.

If only you'd had your camera
they could have stayed forever.

Haybales in Westerwolde

Yellow roller-coasters, sea waves of straw,
not Monet's haystacks
but free-wheeling barrels
strung out in a straight line
diagonal in the field.

Giants must have rolled them there,
and then, after the initial propulsion,
watched them lose momentum
as they idled to a halt.

Wrapped in their cylindrical symmetry
the last glint of the sun's amber
strikes their sides like fire.

Landscape by Fading Light

Once more Cuyp catches the last of the day
drenched in golden light.
Now all the drama is in the sky –
the closing speech before the final curtain.
As the scene fades from view
we can just make out by a knot of trees
two figures walking the fields,
a topography of hedgerows
dividing the land
the possibility of a distant church,
birds heeling home.

Polders

These tracts
of low-lying
land built up
out of the sea

stretching as
far as the eye
can see

are straight,
single-focused
lines

horizon-held
hand-spans
of grids and
sluices

open for
business and
windmills

Running Through Utrecht (I)

Through the counts of Holland, Burgundy dukes,
the Spanish, the French and the Germans,
wealthy merchants and landowners
estates along the *Vecht*
their summerhouses, railings
and luxuriant gardens
escaping towns for country pursuits
a period of contentment in still-life painting
among vases and flowers
easels in rooms with decorative drapes
the countryside for cycling.

Running Through Utrecht (II)

Through the centre of Amersfoort largely still preserved
boathouses built over centuries
border strongholds burned to the ground
smoke sheds, shipyards and fishermen's houses
De Stilj's artistic movement,
Zocher's green designs.

Scoping Dordrecht

City of tides, history and culture
of prosperity over time,
the battle with water calmer now
as you gaze into one of the inner ports
and think that you've seen
through a trick of the light
a gleam of ancient coins.
Caught out, you walk into the *Nieuwkerk*
which, despite its name,
is the oldest building in town.
Once more it is evident
that things are not as they seem.
Getting the measure of the place
is proving to be difficult:
how to weigh its history
before it slips through from your hand

The Drawbridge over the Oude Rijn, Leiden

Its symmetry draws us in –
the horizontal and the vertical –
the moment it tips like weighing scales
either side of the river –
those chains with the pull of industry
building up behind
so that when the bridge is down
there's not a hair's breadth left
for argument between us.

The Girl with the Pearl Earring

- *for Monica Manolachi*

Thursday morning they took the girl with the pearl earring

d
o
w
n
s
t
a
i
r
s

for a period of temporary storage.
Too many people had been looking at her
and she needed a break.
Keeping that gaze for so long
the way Johannes had instructed
was getting to her. After all,
a girl needs to blink now and then.
Once they'd placed her against the wall
she stepped
right out of
the frame,
took off the blue and gold headscarf
and shook down her hair.
Placing the earring

(Johannes had only given her one)
into the box beside her,
she parted her lips as if to say
she needed time to rest.
They told her to take as long as she wanted.

The public would have to wait.

The Lady Looks Out to Sea

In Stavoren,
shielding her eyes from the sun,
all she sees is a storm of yellow stalks
raging in the wind
and out of the wave-glitter
fish breaking the surface
including the one with her ring.
Discovering it at supper one night
she could not have been more surprised.
It was like looking at
the ring of Polycrates
in Herodotus -
history repeating itself over and over.
If only she could change it
she would.

The Lock House, Hindeloopen.

Beyond the closed gates, a vista of masts and rigging,
with drawbridge, dwellings, moored craft,
caulked keels, flat bottom boats at anchor
and the square clock, face to the sun,
placing its hands at ten to four
on an afternoon of quiet repose,
blue-sky thinking, balmy air
taken in May 2016
with your hand-held digital camera:

the *Sylhús* locked in time.

The Martyrdom of St. Boniface

English schoolboys never forgave him for writing the first Latin
grammar
or the pagans for work in the mission field with Willibrord and Wilfred
out and about in Frisia -
a Christian pitched against unbelievers
or was it when he destroyed in public
the oak of Thor at Geismar
(his emblem in art is an axe).
where lateral roots and acorns
set off mass conversions
when everyone expected him to be struck down dead –
maybe it was that
or the entry into the unevangelized north-east flatlands
where Death caught up with him in Dokkum
as he tried to shield himself with a book of texts
hapless against daggers and swords.

The Race on Skates

Forget the axel, the flip and the loop.
Rotational jumps are not in it:
speed skating is what it's about. The art of testing mettle
on iced-over canals or 400 metre tracks circling 100 times.
Knots of them are out there in spandex suits,
protective hats, pads for knees and shins,
competitive to the nth. degree
where n = never give up.

Nine down, two to go.

Back Garden Blues

Aubretia after rain. Small grape hyacinths
flowers conical and hanging
perianth segments almost fused.
Columbine petals with hooked spurs.
Viper's bugloss. Germander speedwell
round-headed rampions and
blue-wave hydrangeas.
Sybil Bradshaw pelargoniums.
Campanula carpatica.
Forking larkspur, Siberian iris.
Calyx-winged spring gentians.
Syringa vulgaris.

How little we know of their world.

Backyard Bees

The day we stumbled on a swarm of bees
all you could think of was
baby-blue berries, batchelor's buttons,
butterflies, buddleias and
billiard-ball blooms.
Babbling brooks and black-eyed beans.
Blackthorn, butterbur and beech bark
bladderwort, bloom-berry and buckbean,
blanched bur-reeds and black bryony,
black bindweed, bay and bogbeans,
blackwort, bridewort and burwort,
borage, brooklime and broomrape,
basil, box and bumble bees.

What's Not to Buy

Painted miniature Delft-blue houses, souvenir dolls in national dress.
Wooden clogs that come in all sizes, red coral Volendam necklaces,
Makkum-in-Friesland earthenware tiles,
Haagse Hopjes coffee-flavoured sweets,
bottles of Amstel Bier,
Zaans mustard,
Roomboter Babbelaars Zeeland butter candies
Jan de Raad's antiques
rounds of Edam cheese.

Already you are opening the clasp on your purse
to make that must-have purchase
while the moment lasts.

Notes and Acknowledgements

Special thanks are due to Sheri Lindner and Paul Surman for their close reading of the manuscript and their respective commentaries on it. Thanks are also due to members of the Burgh Poets, Stirling, for comments on specific poems. It is a pleasure to share poetry with you all.

A Bergen Alphabetum

Ludwig Holberg (1684-1754), writer, essayist, philosopher, historian and playwright, born in Bergen. He is considered to be the founder of modern Danish and Norwegian literature.

Ole Bull (1810-1880), virtuoso violinist and composer, born in Bergen. He took a particular interest in Norwegian folk music.

Bergen Rain

regn (rain), *regnskyll* (downpour), *regnskur* (rain shower).

Stalheim

The Stalheimskleiva road runs up a ridge between two cascading waterfalls and is one of the steepest stretches of road in Northern Europe. On its way to the top, the road winds its way up 13 sharp hairpin bends. The road was built by manual labour between 1842 and 1846 in order to improve the post road between Oslo and Bergen.

Frogner

The sculpture park in the Frogner Park, Oslo, contains more than 200 sculptures by Gustav Vigeland (1869–1943) in bronze, granite and wrought iron. It was installed mainly in the period 1940-1949, but took over 40 years to create. The centrepiece of the whole collection is the monolith which stands at the highest point in the park and measures 17 metres above ground. The sculpture is carved out of one stone block and depicts 121 intertwined human figures, meant to represent the desire of humanity to reach out to the divine. The carving of this monolith took over 14 years and involved work by the artist himself as well as three other stone carvers.

Ulvik

The words in italics are quotations from poems by the horticulturist, translator and poet, Olav H. Hauge (1908-1994) who was a native of Ulvik.

What I Remember about Helsinki

The Stockmann store in the centre of Helsinki is the largest department store in Northern Europe with more than 50,000 square metres of shopping space spread across ten floors.

What I Like about Helsinki Now

I am indebted to Laura Iisalo and Melanie Dower's book 'Helsinki: People Make the City' (Cozy Publishing, 2017) for certain lines in this poem. Reading this book gave me the idea for the poem.

RELANDERSGRUND is the name of an historic lighthouse ship that was built in 1888 and has now been converted into a restaurant.

Postage on this Poem has already been Paid

Oscar Merikanto (1868-1924), Finnish composer, music critic, pianist, and organist.

Armas Järnefelt (1869-1958), Finnish composer and conductor.

Aleksis Kivi Steps Down from His Statue

Aleksis Kivi (1834-1872), Finnish author who wrote the first significant novel in the Finnish language, *Seitsemän veljestä* ("Seven Brothers") in 1870. Today, Kivi's reputation has risen to that of iconic status and his birthday,10 October ,is celebrated as Finnish Literature Day.

The bronze memorial statue, designed and sculpted by Wäinö Aaltonen was unveiled on 10 October, 1939 and is located in the Helsinki Railway Square in front of the Finnish National Theatre. It shows the writer seated on a chair.

Aulis Sallinen Enlarging the World

Aulis Sallinen (b. 1935), Finnish composer. 'Washington Mosaics' is the title of his fifth symphony and 'From A New Zealand Diary' is the title of his sixth symphony.

Thomas Allen Munro Curnow (1911-2001), New Zealand poet and journalist.

I am indebted to liner notes written by Ronald Weitzman relating to Aulis Sallinen's sixth symphony 'From A New Zealand Diary' for some of the wording in this poem.

Gert Mortensen Engaging in a Dialogue with the Malmö Symphony Orchestra

Gert Mortensen (b.1958). One of the leading percussion players in Denmark.

Once again, I am indebted to liner notes written by Ronald Weitzman relating to Aulis Sallinen's second symphony (originally called 'Symphonic Dialogue for Solo Percussion Player and Orchestra) for some of the wording in this poem.

Writ in Nostalgia for Tampere

Viktor Jansson (1886-1958), Finnish sculptor and father of the author Tove Jansson.

Moomins: a reference to the fictional characters created by the writer and illustrator Tove Jansson (1914-2001).

Poem Out of Oulu

Leevi Madetoja (1887-1947), Finnish composer, music critic, conductor and teacher. The poem refers to the second movement of Madetoja's first symphony composed in 1916. Madetoja was born in Oulu but died in Helsinki.

Bosschaert's 'Vase with Flowers'

Ambrosius Bosschaert the Elder (1573-1621), Flemish-born Dutch still life painter and art dealer. He is recognised as one of the earliest painters who created floral still lifes as an independent genre.

Cuyp's Cows

Albrecht Cuyp (1620-1691) was one of the leading Dutch Golden Age painters, producing mainly landscapes. He is especially known for his large views of Dutch riverside scenes in a golden early morning or late afternoon light.

The Lady Looks Out To Sea

The lady in question is the lady of Stavoren whose statue stands in the town square of Stavoren. The poem refers to a Dutch folktale originating from the 16th century which exists in many versions.

The Race on Skates

This poem refers to the tradition of the *'Elfstedentocht'* or 'Eleven Cities Tour', a race for people on ice skates which takes place on canals in Friesland in the north of the Netherlands. The route of the race goes through eleven towns and is nearly 200 kilometres long. It can only be held in winters when it has been cold enough to freeze the canals to a depth safe for skating on.

What's Not to Buy

This is partly a 'found' poem based on a listing in the DK Eye Witness Guide to The Netherlands.

www.ingramcontent.com/pod-product-compliance
Lightning Source LLC
Chambersburg PA
CBHW022203160726
48282CB00024B/305
* 9 7 8 8 1 1 9 2 2 8 7 4 4 *